Noble Brother:
The Story of the Last Prophet in Poetry

Hesham A. Hassaballa

ISBN: 0985326522

ISBN-13: 978-0985326524

DEDICATION

In the Name of the Precious Beloved Lord, the Infinitely Good and Most Graciously Merciful. It is only by His grace that I can do anything in this life.

I also dedicate this work to our beloved Master Muhammad, upon whom God's eternal peace be forever, whose shining light of guidance helps us navigate our way through the darkness of earthly existence.

Finally, I dedicate this work to my beloved wife, without whom I would be forever lost. You have been, and will always be, one of His greatest gifts to me.

CONTENTS

INTRODUCTION

I arrived in Medina, the City of the Holy Prophet (peace be upon him) at 3 AM on February 2nd, 2003. It was during my *Hajj*, or pilgrimage, where – once in their lives – every Muslim must make the journey to Mecca. Visiting his city is not a required part of the *Hajj*, but since pilgrims are already there, they almost always make the journey to visit Medina. As we were being driven towards the city itself, it was so quiet, so peaceful. I felt the smiling presence of the Prophet all around me. I could actually feel him with me, and it was very soothing indeed.

Our hotel, thanks be to the Lord, was very close to the Prophet's Mosque. To our chagrin, however, it had already closed for the night (the mosque is not open 24 hours a day like that Grand Mosque of Mecca). Still, even closed, it was a beautiful sight to behold.

At 9 AM the next morning, I went speedily to the Prophet's Mosque. It was one of the most beautiful I had ever seen; it even rivaled the Grand Mosque in Mecca in its beauty. I felt enormous tranquility in my heart as I walked through its huge pillars and underneath its magnificent arches. My awe, however, was quickly overwhelmed by giddy excitement. All I wanted to do was visit the Prophet's grave. I have read about his life multiple times; I have asked God to send down His blessings upon the Prophet probably tens of thousands of times. Now, finally, it was my chance to stand before him face to face.

By the time I got there, so many people were already crowded around his grave. The closer I came to his grave, however, the happier I felt. I prayed a quick prayer in the area known as the *Rawda*, which according to Tradition is a piece of Paradise on earth. After finishing, I was finally standing "face-to-face" with the Prophet in his grave. The feeling I had was truly indescribable. I greeted him by saying, "Peace be unto you, O Messenger of God." I then added: "Long have I wanted to be with you," and the tears could not stop streaming down my face.

Finally, I was with my beloved. Finally, I stood the closest I have ever been to the Prophet Muhammad. Finally, I had come from so far away to be with the man who had guided every aspect of my life, even though he had died centuries before I was even born.

I wish I could do it all over again, because the feeling I had – though indescribable – was ecstatic nonetheless. No matter who I meet in the future; no matter what long lost friend or relative I may see again, nothing will ever give me the same feeling as I had visiting the Prophet Muhammad in his noble city of Medina. Out of this intense feeling of love for the Prophet, *Noble Brother* was born.

The Prophet's story has been told thousands upon thousands of times, from generation to generation. Scholars have written volumes upon volumes of books and compendia about his amazing life and ministry. Lecturers and Professors have spoken about him for hours and hours. Poets have sung his praises throughout the ages. Even his most ardent enemies today have spent many an hour and day speaking about him. Yet, rarely have I seen his entire life story told exclusively in poetry. Thus, I had decided to write it myself.

Noble Brother, now in its second edition, tells the beautiful story of the Prophet's life and ministry in a very unique way. To those familiar with his story, the historical events surrounding each poem may be clear. Yet, not everyone – including many Muslims – is intimately familiar with the story of the Prophet's life. Thus, with each poem comes a brief historical background that will give meaning to the poem's individual style and manner of recounting the specific part of the Prophet's life. These background pieces are listed in the back of the book in the Appendix. The way I suggest the Appendix be used is this: the poem should be read first, and the reader should see if he or she can figure out the story behind it. If the story is still elusive, then the reader should consult the Appendix.

Indeed, these poems and their background stories are not meant to be an academic historical recounting of the Prophet's biography. Yet, it should give the reader a general overview of the Prophet's life, and it is hoped that, after reading *Noble Brother,* the reader will learn more about the Prophet Muhammad from reputable sources. To that end, I have included a suggested reading list for those readers who want to learn more.

Yet, the magnanimity of the Prophet Muhammad's

life lies not only in the historical events surrounding him, but also in his character. His wife A'isha (may God be pleased with her) once described him as a "Qur'an walking on earth." The Lord our God spoke about him thus: "For, behold, you [stand] on an exalted standard of character." (68:4)

Thus, in this newest edition of *Noble Brother*, there is a second part of the book that has a never-before published poem, in the form of an epic, recounting specific stories of the Prophet Muhammad's truly awe-inspiring character. Again, at the end of the epic, there will be a brief historical background explaining the history behind it. Along with the new poems in this second edition, some of the previous poems have been changed slightly for style and flow.

It is my hope and prayer that everyone who reads this book of poetry learns more about the Prophet Muhammad and comes to love him as deeply and sincerely as I do. It is my hope and prayer that, with this book, I can help bring about mutual understanding between faith communities and the human family at large. Moreover, it is my hope and prayer that you, dear reader, will enjoy reading this book as much as I have enjoyed writing it.

PART ONE: HIS LIFE

Brutality and a New Dawn

HESHAM A. HASSABALLA

The sun was hot and bright, yet darkness abounds
The wind was hot, yet cold was all around
A land so holy from the very start of time
Became of shame, with righteousness unable to climb

The sands upon which the Patriarch tread
Became poisoned with the blood of innocent dead
The House that the Patriarch built with devoted son
Became crowded with wooden god, one by one

Barbarians roamed the land, free to brutalize
Upon the weak and helpless, the strong capitalized
War and counter-war was the rule of the day
Distorting the Sacred Months to have their way

Wealth and usury used as a vicious ploy
To dominate, enslave, brutalize, and destroy
And the innocent child is suffocated with sand
Because she is who she is, insanity filled the land

There were some who called to the way of the One
Yet their call was mocked, their purpose undone
Hopeless, it seemed, for the state of their souls
And slowly did they slip toward suffering untold

But hope was at hand, a New Dawn was near
And all was not lost to terror and fear
For due to the prayer of the Patriarch so clear
A Noble Caller to God's way will soon appear

Year of the Elephant

HESHAM A. HASSABALLA

A dispute among the sons of Abyssinia raged
A grand drama of epic proportion was staged
In a land far away from the plain of Paran
Where injustice and brutality freely ran

A king was incensed by an apparent act
Of disloyalty and rebellion to keep peace intact
But his deputy stressed that his allegiance was true
So, listen to what he set out to do

A church, he built, truly grand in its scale
Large were its steeples, enormous beyond the pale
The skill of his act did not fail or falter
Thus, he wanted the Arabs to venerate its altar

But come they did not, them he could not persuade
To forsake the Ancient House the Patriarch made
And to show his distaste, a Bedouin treks to its walls
And defiles it with his filth in an act of gall

Enraged became the General at the brazen stain
And it lead to an idea that was most insane
"Destroy, I will, that House they so revere.
So that they will be forced to come and worship
here!"

An army was dispatched from where he stood
Which he led himself, because he could
And mighty elephants were put at the helm
So that the Ancient House could be overwhelmed

NOBLE BROTHER

Reached it they did, but the people did flee
To watch what would become of the insolent army
The elephants refused to destroy sacred brick
And from a distance came birds, without sword or
stick

And the General was pursued by stone small as pea
And his army decimated and forced to flee
And the House was saved by its Guardian Lord
From the arrogant rage of the invading horde

Yet this miraculous battle was not the greatest gift
To a people desperate for faith and spiritual uplift
For in that very year happened a glorious thing
To a poor widow was born a majestic king

A Sacred Union

NOBLE BROTHER

A sacred union was ordained from above
Two souls joined in dignity and love
A child was conceived by the blessed pair
But father passed away before he could see his heir

The burden was light for now widowed mother
Who has to carry child without support of father
A voice came to her in the dark of night
Showing her palaces from afar with a glorious light

The light emanates from her womb which holds
A special child, about whom tales will be told
And the voice instructs her to ask the Only
To seek refuge in Him from both envier and envy

The glorious day comes and the star is shone
A glorious blessing from the Lord of the Throne
"He has come!" shouts the follower from before
And expectations are high from palaces galore

Nobleman become father lifts up the child in glee
And declares to the world that "Most Praised is he"
And now the time has come for all of the world
To worship the One and Only, Our Most Beloved
Lord

They Passed Him By

NOBLE BROTHER

One by one, they passed him by
In the heat and sun, the left him lay
"An orphan," would they sadly sigh
"How much, really, can his mother pay?"

When come, they did, to seek a child
Slow and weak was their feeble beast
Delayed and detained were they mile after mile
Could not keep up with the group in the least

But they came away with empty hand
Nothing to show for their long journey
Yet they did not want to return to their barren land
With the very same hands, dusted and empty

"Let us go back," said they to one another
"Let us take that orphan whom we left at first."
"He may be blessed even if he is without father.
An orphan may not be such a terrible curse."

And the blessings came as a nourishing rain
Giving strength and zeal to once feeble mule
To the amazement of all, dead turned to fruited plain
And plenty after little became the regular rule

One by one, they passed him by
In the heat and sun, the left him lay
But little did they know that there lie
A Holy Messenger from the One on High

The Boy and the Monk

NOBLE BROTHER

He clung to his leg, begging to go
A favorite son, although his father has passed
To Syria he goes on the ancient caravan flow
So he finally gives in, as son's persistence lasts

Travel they did, heat of brutal sun bearing down
Always difficult it is, to trek the sands of the isle
Yet on the son, heat did not make him frown
For there was a cloud sent to follow all the while

Scholar and scribe has a long time ignored
The countless caravans passing by this place
Yet now, suddenly, he earnestly implored
Young and old to eat, drink, and enjoy his grace

He looked earnestly at the child, looking for the Sign
And he asked the young boy in the name of their god
"Do not ask me that!" he replied, for this did malign
His Maker and Shaper, the Only Glorious Living God

"So I ask you in God's Name," was the monk's reply
Amazed at the young boy's blazing faith and grace
He examined his back and then beheld it with a sigh
The Mark of the Chosen, in its prophesied place

Home, the boy went, straight away without delay
Fear for his safety filled the scholar and scribe
For if he was discovered after deciding to stay
Killed would he have been, without help from tribe

He Came to Town One Day

NOBLE BROTHER

He came to town one day, offering his insight
Declaring to fathers their sons' possible glory
A future declared to be grim or bright
Using an ancient art to tell a story

He looked here and there at child's face
And gave out his forecast to smiling sire
Yet, eyes became fixed as a lover's embrace
When he first beheld this face, lighted as fire

Guardian's glee turns quickly to fear
When sage's gaze would not leave
So guardian took his boy away from here
To protect brother's son and give him reprieve

But sage shouted: "Where is that boy I saw?
Bring him back so I can see him here!
For by my knowledge and by my law
Great he will be! For him, all will cheer!"

Noble Brother

NOBLE BROTHER

A stop on the way from strife to liberty
Two noble men require rest and tranquility
Hospitality is asked of a woman most cunning
To give them respite after constant running

"No request is needed, had we possessed to give.
Honoring our guest is the way we live."
A miracle was revealed and hunger eschewed
Awe was inspired and blessings imbued

Then she described the Noble Brother
A description unlike any other
Down through the ages her story survived
To keep the image of the Emissary alive

A beautiful man with shining face
Goodly built, his body full of grace
Balanced and normal, was he, in totality
Neither large nor small, voice full of humility

A long neck and full beard wholly embraced
Eyes deep and black, full brow enlaced
Silence brings a man composed and stately
His speech does not fail to impress greatly

From afar his beauty strikes the beholder
Yet when near, he captivates the holder
His speech is sweet as the honey of the bee
Neither lacking nor given all too freely

The love for him flows like a river in rage
Life for him is fully and willingly waged
A man whose nobility can almost sing
A man who will, one day, be a noble king

The Honest One

NOBLE BROTHER

He grows up in purity, free from the smears
Of passion and folly, he needs not to shed tears
Of regret for succumbing to the needs of the beast
Which resides inside, not a friend in the least

Slumber would overtake him whenever he thinks
To indulge in passion, play, indecency, or drink
A day of heat, and to disrobe they proposed
But he fell to the ground so that he is not exposed

The Holy House has fallen into disarray
The foundations broken in a terrible display
A pledge was made to rebuild the Shrine
So that Sacred Precinct can once again shine

The stones were cleared, the dust was cleaned
The new House built and its stability gleaned
Together do the tribes work, sweat, and stand
To witness the glory of the Lord at hand

Yet now comes the absolute and greatest task
And forever in honor does the doer bask
To set the Black Stone in its holy place
Led the brothers to fall from their exalted place

Each tribe had pledged to bathe in blood
A barbarian standoff risking sanguineous flood
Every side now vowing to set the great stone
Their ugly sides now completely bare and shown

A compromise was struck to put violence at bay
"Let him who enters this gate save the day."
And when they beheld him, they erupted in glee
"With the Honest One, we are all very happy!"

Bring them together, he did, with poise and grace
And averted a bloodbath in a most sacred place
A foreshadowing of this noble man's future glory
Beautiful it is, how goes this noble man's story

A Love Story

HESHAM A. HASSABALLA

Handsome, honorable, and honest was he
Full of beauty, grace, poise, and civility
Respected by all and disgraced by none
A great future was in store for this favorite son

Beautiful, graceful, and noble was she
And wealthy with much means and more than plenty
Three times in the bonds of marriage did she comply
But now renouncing that bond as the years went by

And then she saw him and impressed was she
By his aura, his stature, and his impeccable honesty
And so she sent word to him to enter her employ
To further her trade and give him a job to enjoy

Blessed was he on his very first mission
Enthralled was his companion as he rode with him
Gentle and kind, and his character altogether sweet
And cloud would follow to shade them from the heat

A master merchant he proved to be
Buying and selling to profit doubly
And when he returned to the city of his employer
The story of his grace did not fail to enthrall her

And so the embers of love began to burn once more
And she felt a strong bond like she did once before
And so sent an emissary to test the willingness
Of the Honest One for a trial of wedded bliss

Astounded was he at the sacred request
It was a humble response to a glorious inquest
"Leave it to me," was the confident reply
To the man who agreed and happily complied

NOBLE BROTHER

And a happy house was nurtured and formed
For noble man and woman agreed to conform
To the ancient path of Father and Mother
And the House of the Trustworthy was like no other

Retreat to the Cave

NOBLE BROTHER

Though the years were kind to his blessed soul
The world and its tribulations took a tremendous toll
Justice offended, and the well of mercy had gone dry
Unheeded went the desperate and terrified cry

Reflect, did he, over the state of all things
And the terrible fury with which injustice stings
How He Whose Light over everything shone
Was replaced by creations of wood and stone

A happy life he was given quite freely
A beautiful wife and children he loved dearly
Yet, something troubled his pure and white soul
And as the passed, it took a larger toll

The darkness of the times suffocated his heart
And the stench of iniquity pushed him far apart
And so he forsook home and loving spouse
To contemplate in silence, with view of Holy House

More and more days did he spend alone
More brightly the light of his heart had shone
And soon an event that would shape the world
Would come flying to him and hope will unfurl

Soon would he know his purpose most true
And his importance he heretofore never knew
Soon would he behold in all glory and power
The Holy Spirit declaring to all the glorious hour

Once Upon a Powerful Night

NOBLE BROTHER

It came once upon a Powerful Night
When, in blink of an eye, darkness became light
And one who was alone on mount and in cave
Felt the presence of the Holy Spirit, and this message
it gave:

"Read!"

Terror and fear filled the pure vessel of his soul
Complete surprise at His method to enroll
"I cannot read," was his most honest reply
Yet the Messenger had no choice but to comply

Squeeze and compress was the Spirit's next act
And the Beloved thought that death was his, in fact
"Read!" once again the Holy Spirit implored
After he released him and to him his breath restored

"I cannot read," was the terrified response
From a pure soul who could not lie, even once
And fierce again did the Spirit compress and squeeze
Taking all breath and in terror did he freeze

"I cannot read," the shaken uttered once more
The same honest reply given as it was before
Holy Spirit took the Noble One in strong embrace
And then unleashed the words of the One with grace

And as the Spirit gave the Message as he did before
Into the Messenger's heart, the Word of the Lord tore
And from that day forth, we have been forever saved
By one single word into a pure heart engraved

And despite all the terror, fear, and fright
And the experience that baffled sense and sight
Our Beloved did not waver, though he did take flight
For it came once upon a Powerful Night

"Cover Me!"

Running, he was, running in fear
Running, he was, away from mount and cave
Fleeing, he was, full of terror that was sheer
Fleeing, he was, afraid that he could be a knave

In shock, he was, from what had just transpired
In shock, he was, from the power of His Spirit
Awed, he was, from His Word Inspired
Awed, he was, that he could not run from it

"Cover Me!": This was his call
"Cover Me!": He beseeched in fear
"Cover Me!": To she who broke his fall
"Cover Me!": His need for her was sincere

Trembling and shaking under cover of love
She was the first from whom he sought aid
Worried that he was forsaken from above
Yet her love and assurance became his shade

"Nonsense!" was her confident reply
"Our Lord could never leave you afflicted.
For you always answer the terrified cry
Do not, dear heart, be about this conflicted!"

A Scribe of the Book did she then seek out
One with bonds of kinship strong
Recounted story further assuaged all doubt
That he was the Messenger, awaited all along

And so set was the stage for a new beginning
The Messenger being prepared for his task
Madness is not his, and he stopped running
The world awaits God's light from his flask

First Call

A morning like any other in heat and sun
And up the familiar mount climbs a favorite son
His noble voice sails over wind and breeze
To tell a new news of such important degree

The people hearken to his honest call
And they listen intently, one and all
"If I told you an army was behind this mount,
Would you believe me my factual account?"

"Yes, by God!" was their unanimous reply
"For we have never known you, our son, to lie."
And thus he began his noble creed and task
And to follow him to Paradise is all he asked

"May you perish!" was the response of his kin
The brother of his father did angrily chime in
And dispersed the crowd from hearing his call
And dissuaded from the message one and all

And thus begins the endless fight
Between forces of darkness and those of light
At every turn of this most holy place
Does his kith and kin rear his ugly face

And turn away every soul he can find
From the Messenger who simply wants to remind
That there is a consequence to act and deed
And turn to the Lord if you want to be freed

But his enemies grew in number and guile
And torture and murder was their typical style
To try to prevent more from entering the fold
Of a faith and creed that was earlier foretold

NOBLE BROTHER

But the Noble One persisted in his sacred quest
And never did he waiver, falter, or rest
For the Word of the Lord must reign supreme
Even if it meant he would face evil in extreme

Flight to the King

NOBLE BROTHER

Slow but sure did grow the Messenger's call
Fast and swift did come his enemies' gall
And as the flock grew in number all the while
So did the treachery and torture and guile

Thus did the Messenger sadly send away
Kith and kin to a land where their fears allay
And where they are foreign, they will surely find
A King who just, honorable, fair, and kind

Swiftly, though, the plan did the enemy discover
And quickly they sent friend of the King to recover
A brilliant emissary who sought to return
The believers to the city where they all will burn

"We are kin!" declared the Messenger's blood
"We bow to the same God," Master of the flood
So proof of their divine call was thus demanded
And Word of God the Companion then handed

Verse upon verse spoke of the Blessed Mother
Who gave birth to a child without need of father
And after silence brought by the power of His Word
Tears wet the King's face from what he had heard

He turns to friend tasked with bringing them back
To say that he would never let them be attacked
And so the noble kith and kin were given leave to stay
In the land of the Believing King until an appointed
day

The Hunter Submits

NOBLE BROTHER

Around the Holy House would he softly walk
Venerating the Shrine which his father built
Neither would he curse nor even quickly talk
To the vermin who sat and hurled their filth

Around and around the ancient cube did he go
Without even looking in their cursed direction
Answer he did not, though his face did show
Distaste at their curses and their malediction

Silently did he walk away from the Holy House
They thought, in their vanity, that they won the day
But little did they know that they now did rouse
An ancient ally with a strength it would display

Word quickly reached the Hunter of Lions
Champion of his Noble House and Line
Enraged became he when he had heard the lines
Of derision and guile, with a response declined

Forthwith the Hunter ran to the Sacred Precinct
To answer the call of the Father of Ignorance
Anger and violence was indeed his instinct
And Hunter answered with mind of vengeance

Strike, did he, at the top of his countenance
Blood streaking down the repugnant soul
"Do you dare attack him who has much grace?
When my faith and heart is under his control?"

Shock and awe filled all those who had heard
These words spoken in anger and complete haste
And now spread like fire did this new word
That in the One, the Hunter's faith is now based

Comprehend not, did he, when he thought at first
At the words that he had hurled at the enemy
But to go back now would be nothing but the worst
And then did true faith replace previous ignominy

And into smiling eyes did he go to embrace
The noble son of brother whom he swore to defend
And now would his life be full of the Lord's grace
When he became loyal Companion until the very end

"Today I am Going to Kill This Man!"

HESHAM A. HASSABALLA

Today I am going to kill this man!
Who has usurped truth for his arrogant plan
Today I am going to kill this man!
For his pathetic claim that God is not man

Tear asunder the ties of family did he
With his "words of God" that are so silly
For him, our kin left on horse and caravan
So today I am going to kill this man!

Here is my sword, sharpened and ready
My resolve is strong, my hand is steady
Nothing will stop me fulfilling my plan
Today I am going to kill this man!

I was on my way to the accursed's locale
Fast was my pace, higher my morale
I was stopped by someone that I knew
Who saw on my face glee eschewed

"Where are you headed, in such anger?
What could cause you so much rancor?"
"The flames of evil, he does repeatedly fan.
So today I am going to kill this man!"

"Not so fast, O Angered Lion!
Stop and see the end of your line.
Clean up your own house before you strike,
For your own kin follows whom you do not like!"

"Treachery! Brigands! Infidels!" I raged
I am wild as a beast, hopelessly caged
Straightaway to her house, I quickly ran
To see this disaster in my house firsthand

NOBLE BROTHER

I could not believe what I was told
That my own blood had left our fold
A strange murmur behind her door I heard
And burst in her home to hear this word

"Did you leave the way of our fathers?!" I riled
"And leave our people and traditions defiled?!"
Rather than calm, my actions were instead
A vicious blow that drew blood from her head

She fell to the ground, and her head was bleeding
'Twas an act of shame, unbecoming of my breeding
"Let me read the words I heard before my strike,
And I swear I will not do anything you do not like."

"Go and wash: you are defiled by faith in stone."
And the water did calm the rage my face had shown
When I read the Words, written on parchment I held
Thunder clapped in my soul, and I nearly fell

"Where is the son of the servant of God?" I did ask
For there was one thing on my mind, only one task
I ran steadily to his secret abode without delay
And neither did I waiver, nor off the path did I stray

And when I entered and saw his face, full of beauty
I fell to the ground for his power was too weighty
And when he asked me to answer his noble call
I declared my faith in God and him before one and all

Joyous glee filled the air and also my heart
And from then on, never were we apart
In the morning, I swore that I would kill this man
Yet, blessed was I that God had a different plan

Enemy's Plan

NOBLE BROTHER

Try, they did, to stem the tide of his call
Try, they did, to kill them one and all
Try, they did, to thwart or even dispel
But they could not stop the growing swell

Day by day grew the number of faithful
More and more did their numbers swell
The rage and guile of the enemy did grow
And to oppose him, they lined up in rows

Gather, they did, at the Sacred House
Find, they did, a way to finally oust
That noble son, whom they detest
And hate more than all the rest

And so, they did, plan and plot and think
Their minds, they did, strain to the brink
Then in their brains did they carve
A plan to choke, stifle, and starve

Thus, they did, gather all of his kin
To deprive them until bone and skin
To a deserted valley did they marshal
And boycott kith and kin, one and all

Year upon year of trial did pass
A cruel punishment and moral morass
Then at last the Lord did finally break
The plan with not even a small quake

The parchment upon which ink did spill
In order to starve and perish and kill
Was destroyed by a tiny speck of creature
His power was stronger than their feature

And so the Messenger was finally free
His kith and kin were filled with glee
They planned and plotted and tried to dispel
But they could not stop the Messenger's swell

Year of Sadness

HESHAM A. HASSABALLA

Dark were these days for the Beloved
Sadness filled the thoughts of his head
Relentless was the guile of the enemy
Not one minute would they let him be free

Three years did he starve, thirst, and suffer
To empty his hope and deplete his coffer
And even though it did not bear fruit
Soon more sadness would come to boot

Companion and mother and friend was she
Who filled his heart with love and tranquility
When all the other lights did go out
Never did she falter or ever feel doubt

But now his life was dealt a terrible blow
For to her Lord did his beloved wife go
And pain did pierce his beautiful heart
For from his true love, he would now have to part

And the tears of his loss would barely become dry
When another test would come from On High
His trusted advocate through thick and thin
Would also, from sheer brutality, be done in

Alas he was now without comfort and protector
Vulnerable to new levels of guile and rancor
Now even the weak and feeble would mock
And throw dust, stone, blood, and rock

Yet, as always, never was he truly alone
For he had a light that always shone
For the True Lord was always there
To help lighten the burden he had to bear

NOBLE BROTHER

So soon would he see his noble station
And how his story would be true inspiration
For the Great One would never abandon
The truthful, honest, and noble son

Second City

NOBLE BROTHER

Utterly rejected by his own kith and kin
In terror was the state of the noble mission
Many believers did they torture and slay
And many others they forced to flee far away

The Noble Brother did not waiver or falter
And not one iota of His Word did he alter
Yet the pressure of the enemy did not relent
And for their taunts and threats, they did not repent

All hope was lost for the people of this City
That they would believe and attain felicity
And thus to the Southeast did the Messenger move
To invite the Second City to makes its faith improve

"We reject you and your faith!" was their rude reply
And a horrible thing they ordered from on high
Street urchin and child did they send on his way
To stone his feet for his request to stay

Blood and dirt did stream and defile
His noble feet as they stoned all the while
And flee for his life, the Messenger was compelled
And beneath a tree he laid, as a warrior felled

And toward the Heaven did his noble face turn
To beseech the Beloved for their ugly spurn
"To Thee I complain of my weakness," he cried
And he spoke to the Lord without one tittle of pride

He sought refuge in the Light of the Face of the Lord
From His anger; for with God, he had no discord
And upon the Messenger, God's mercy did descend
And evil did not become the Emissary's end

Arise, O Gallant Son

NOBLE BROTHER

Arise, O gallant and noble one
Arise, O Messenger and noble son
Arise, for your Lord has heard your plea
And your faithful call full of humility

Arise, and come with me, your powerful guide
And ride on this steed with enormous stride
Tonight you will leave your place of sleep
From Holy House to the Wall where they weep

In the flash of an eye does he arrive
On the plain where the Prophets came alive
And take his place at the head of the row
To lead the Leaders, standing toe to toe

A choice he is given: which should he drink?
Immediately does he choose, not needing to think
When milk and wine is offered to the Master
He chooses the milk, and his people prosper

And now, noble son, the time has arrived
To go to the One, who made you come alive
Up toward the heavens does he steadily climb
The laws of heaven and earth stop, as does time

At each heavenly gate, he is warmly greeted
Never is he abandoned or ever defeated
A dignified visitor has for the first time graced
The Seven Heavens and is always embraced

Until he reaches the Highest Station
Higher than any man from any nation
To the Lote Tree was he faithfully guided
By the Holy Spirit, where whose power subsided

HESHAM A. HASSABALLA

Humbly there, he stood before the One
Whose Light shines brighter than the Sun
In reverence did he greet the Lord on High
And with the Creator's Word did he comply

Fifty prayers did the Beloved request
Of all the believers, as a holy request
And faithfully did the Messenger Obey
Waiver he did not; "No" he did not say

And soon came a holy intercession
From a blessed brother of a brother nation
"Ask to reduce the number of the sacred tally
For to this, your people will fail to rally."

And so he went back to the Lord on High
To finally reduce the number to five
Then the Messenger left the Holy Presence
And returned to the world with no hesitance

So enthralled and energized by his journey
He realized how truly to the Lord he was worthy
And though he was yet in the midst of darkness
The Precious Lord blessedly showed him bliss

The Pledge

HESHAM A. HASSABALLA

Darkness surrounded him in all its weightiness
But for God, he would crush under its loneliness
It seemed that lost was all hope for God's cause
And Defeat had surrounded him with its jaws

Yet in that darkness came the light of the Sun
And the hope that, at long last, God's will is done
A band of people from a faraway land
Came to the Prophet to extend a hand

They have come to believe in the Prophet's way
They no longer desired to be led astray
By the ways and traditions of their past
They wished for true salvation that would last

Pledged their lives, their wealth and their blood
Pledged to defend him from the enemy's flood
"Come to us, and we will defend you.
The time has come to be given your due."

Accept their pledge he did with grace
Warmly did he receive the City's embrace
To the North he ordered the faithful to go
To escape the claws of the enemy's death throe

And so, one by one, in secret did they flee
To a strange land, yet with peace and security
Except a former enemy, who issued a dare
And left in the light of day, in the Sun's glare

The Prophet stayed behind until all was clear
His people to safety he dutifully steered
Then chose a companion for his sacred flight
Who wept in happiness, not fear or fright

NOBLE BROTHER

All the while, the enemy did solemnly swear
Planned and plotted, thinking he was unaware
A dagger from every tribe would pierce his chest
To end his life and put his call to final rest

One by one, they stood outside his domicile
To shed his blood and unleash their guile
Yet fail did their plan, for he had by his side
The Lord on High as Protector and Guide

Over many days and many a cool night
The Messenger and Companion did take flight
And on the blessed day he came into the city
The inhabitants sang with joy and felicity

Now a new era in his holy life had begun
After the darkness, now shone forth the Sun
Though from Mecca's hate, he was forced to flee
Yathrib had now become the Enlightened City

Joyous Welcome

NOBLE BROTHER

The Sun is hot and beats down relentless
The desert can be fierce and wholly heartless
Anticipation is high among the people of the town
Enough to keep in the Sun, father of frown

All are out, awaiting the sacred visitor
They are all talking, and their faces are eager
They are about to give up hope for another day
When they hearken two small figures far away

The figures grow larger as the heat bears down
Joy and elation replace scowl and frown
And as the holy one approaches the City
Voices of song erupt in joyous felicity

They rhyme of the coming of the white moon
His arrival is hailed as a most welcome boon
"At last, the Messenger to us has come!
At last, our Leader and his Victors are one!"

All hands reach out to take his rein
Even those whose love is only feigned
Yet, the Noble Brother tells all to leave her be
For she is guided by the One in Unity

His camel walks freely, choosing the sacred place
Where he will live and make a prayer space
At speed they merrily embark to erect
The mosque which they must make correct

Even before this sacred deed is complete
To his followers are noble exhortations replete
Urging peace, love, brotherhood, and charity
And the end will be Paradise, Land of Felicity

HESHAM A. HASSABALLA

The House is built, and the task is now done
To this place, must all the believers run
Yet, the happiness of this City will be short
For they have yet a vicious enemy to retort

Enemies Make War

Rage! Fury! Anger was the scream!
Men from the North ruined their dream
The son whom they tried and failed to eradicate
Now became King of a brand new State

Teeth and hands were angrily clenched
Thirst for blood not easily quenched
Gather, they did, at the Sacred Precinct
To chart a plan, swift and succinct

"Renegades they are, and fools are we.
To allow them to slip away so easily.
To answer this act of war, so fiendish
We grasp their treasures and arms we brandish."

And so they did seize all that had value
Confiscate all fabric of every color and hue
To line their caravans with wealth that was stolen
To line their pockets with a greed emboldened

Shock grew throughout the Enlightened City
Over this egregious act of ignominy
Now the Prophet took matters in hand
To reclaim their wealth all over the land

A caravan of Mecca, large in its bounty
Was passing near by the Prophet's City
A small band of believers did the Prophet send
To take back the wealth that was with evil in blend

Screams of war flew back to the enemy
Men of arms came to spare no pity
Teeth and hands were angrily clenched
Thirst for blood not easily quenched

NOBLE BROTHER

March to the North to wipe out his band
And end the Prophet's call in the land
A reluctant war right there was waged
With uneven numbers violently engaged

Two hours of the cry and the angry shout
Was all they needed for a complete rout
Mighty Mecca fled here and there
To shock, awe, and intractable despair

Now the world knows that this man is real
With a Lord and resolve much stronger than steel
And the "pitiful band" that fled for limb and life
Filled all of Mecca with fear and strife

Brutal Vengeance

NOBLE BROTHER

Egos have been terribly bruised
Enemies become wholly enthused
Wounds are being dressed and tended
Rage and anger becomes distended

Screams and wails over the lost
Despair over the enormous cost
New plans are already being hatched
And a new army will be dispatched

Swords sharpened, spears at the ready
Their march is swift; their feet are steady
With sheer rancor they march once more
To stain with blood, guile, and gore

The City of Light hears the drums of war
And gathers to discuss what is in store
Despite misgivings of the Praised One
They decide to meet the enemy head on

Mecca marches to wreak destruction
The Prophet steadily makes preparations
To the Archers: an order not to leave
No matter the image the eyes receive

The battle goes well for the City of Light
Mecca is quickly put to flight
Yet the Archers now disobey his command
And left the mount to grab booty in hand

From the jaws of a most certain defeat
A future believer leaps to his feet
Seeking to gain from disobedience
He turns on the Prophet with horse and lance

HESHAM A. HASSABALLA

"Muhammad is dead!" was the hue and cry
Crushing the believers with this cruel lie
And the party who was the helm of victory
Succumbs to chaos, defeat, and trickery

Yet alive was he, although bled his wounds
His "death" was simply a weakened swoon
To rally to his side he called the faithful
And brought security to the fearful

And as the believers recovered on the mount
The enemy mutilates all they could count
None was spared from vicious brutality
Even the Hunter was denied his dignity

Mecca leaves the scene in her bloody glow
The believers suffer a terrible blow
Yet their swords will not yet become sheathed
For their enemy's rage has not yet been relieved

Final Blow

"We will end this menace once and for all!
We will strike at the man and make him fall!
This man has eluded for far too long!
Let us overwhelm him with an angry throng!

We will end this menace once and for all!
Our gods once more will we install!
Gather, we will, all those who bear arms!
To bring forth our host and bring him harm!"

The news reached the Prophet in his City
He knew they would come in total hostility
"Stay in the City," was the quick reply
"They will not breach it, however they may try."

Another plan hatched to defend kith and kin
A moment of clarity among the nervous din
A trench was dug as the Persians were wont
A brand new trick to bring about détente

Ten thousand strong came the army of Paran
To destroy the faith, the city, and its Holy Man
Glee in their faces was barely concealed
For their coming feast of blood congealed

A scroll was signed when the Prophet arrived
With People of the Book, so the city could thrive
Defend, they must, in times of danger and war
And this pledge he renewed to protect their door

Then came Mecca with all her hubris
Yet the sight of the trench took away their bliss
For days, they were thwarted by a hole in the earth
And their victory was far and their kills at a death

NOBLE BROTHER

Yet all was not well in the City of Light
For there were enemies within and in plain sight
Hypocrites withdrew to weaken the Lord's band
Traitors conspired to shed blood in the land

Sight became foggy and hearts leapt into the throat
Enemy continued to breach the waterless moat
The small band of believers never wavered one bit
And defended to no end with their prayers split

When hope was dark, there came a glimmer of light
A new wrinkle comes into this deathly fight
An enemy in the ranks now changes his heart
And comes to the City for a brand new start

"I offer my service, Precious Man of the Lord."
"Please," he said, "break this malicious horde."
And so he set forth with a lie in hand
To shake the evil conspiring band

And final blow to the City was thwarted
Victory from an unlikely place was handed
Then came God's Soldier on noble steed
To finish off this most diabolical deed

A cold and unrelenting wind did strike
Extinguishing fire and upending tent spike
And though the believers were not spared its bite
The enemy was smothered with cold and fright

And thus was the enemy's host destroyed
By Plan of the Lord, most cunningly employed
Believers' faces now shone in light
Hypocrites and Traitors now shook in fright

Thus ended the era of war and attack
Mecca's power now seriously cracked
Never again would the Prophet lie in wait
For his enemy to viciously determine his fate

Pilgrimage

HESHAM A. HASSABALLA

The effects of the Trench were felt far and wide
Enemies wont to strike fell with swift stride
The tide has turned for the son of God's slave
A burning faith in the hearts of men is engraved

A dream visits the Messenger by night
A dream that brings to all pure delight
Heads will be shaven after they make the rounds
Shouts of glory for the Lord abound

They set off into the desert, unarmed yet strong
Singing God's praise in beautiful song
Encamped, they were, beyond the Sacred Line
Not to move further as commanded the Divine

The enemy resisted, filled with arrogant pride
Anger and disdain in their hearts did collide
To the Noble Emissary they did say:
"You will not enter His House this day!"

One by one, noblemen seek to understand:
"Why have you come here and made this stand?"
Yet to every man was this single reply:
"We wish to visit the House of the Lord On High!"

In a terrible state were the Lords of Paran
For they could not stop the power of this man
Then the Diplomat they send to etch out a screed
And make peace between these enemies of creed

The terms were set and the truce was signed
And it denied the vision and the Prophet's design
Anger welled in the camp of the Truthful
And their disobedience left the Prophet woeful

NOBLE BROTHER

As they returned to the City with empty hand
It seemed their enemies had prevailed in the land
Yet the Lord sent the Prophet an uplifting decree
That he was given a truly manifest victory

One by one, the Companions came to see
That blessings came out of alleged calamity
The truce they thought would beat God's man
Was in truth the end of the rule of Paran

Vile Betrayal

NOBLE BROTHER

"Yes, there is peace between us and they
But upon our enemies, we will surely prey
We will use this time to gather our rage
And against the Rebel we will firmly engage

Our swords and spears are at the ready
Our breath is silent, our hands are steady
The peace we signed was only a ruse
Live with him? We adamantly refuse!

We don't want peace with this man
We abhor his alleged 'Divine Plan'
We will run him through with sword in hand
And abolish his faith forever from the land

His allies will be shown no quarter or mercy
His friends will be our slaves, never to be set free
Even if they were within the Sacred Line
We will cut them down to pieces fine!"

Murder within the Precincts they most surely did
And after their calumny, they quickly hid
For they knew that retribution will quickly appear
For the treachery committed without shame or fear

News of blood spilt reached holy ears
Shock and anger prevailed over tears
The Faithful gathered in a legion without end
To march upon Mecca in support of friend

A plea for calm passed unheeded
Everyone knew Mecca was defeated
People fled in every direction in fear
Of a terrible vengeance perceived as near

Yet the blood split was hardly a drop
For the man who was coming wanted to stop
The old cycle of blood and violence and war
The old ways of their gods would be no more

He entered the city with head bowed in humility
Thankful to the Lord for his manifest victory
And to those whose crimes were most ferocious
The Noble Brother extended a hand most gracious

Then the gods that stood along House so holy
The gods that stood for generations so boldly
Came tumbling down and turned into dust
When touched by the one who had God's trust

Then the people came into His fold in waves
Delegations and emissaries from every enclave
Came to profess their faith in God the One
And followed the Messenger, shining like the Sun

And as the Prophet returned to his blessed City
The Lord inspired his reflection on this victory
To praise and thank the One With Kindness
And then seek His Undying Mercy and Forgiveness

Final Admonition

The land has been calmed, the storm has passed
No longer are the believers attacked and harassed
The Lord has prevailed over the idols of stone
And the light of His emissary has brightly shone

Now with thousands upon thousands galore
The Noble Brother comes to Mecca once more
Not as conqueror, humble and grateful
But as a pilgrim with the rest of the faithful

He descends upon the Precinct with his divine spark
To walk the paths and the ways of the Patriarch
Around the shrine and between the mounts he goes
And on the pillars, dozens of stones he throws

Then he gathers the faithful at the Plain of Knowing
Turning to the people with his wisdom flowing
He stands before them to give this final creed
And he urges those present and absent to heed

He praises the Lord in His Light and Glory
This was the beginning of his every single story
He reminds the people that this day is sacred
That for a higher purpose were they raised and bred

"You will meet your Lord," was his honest call
"He will reckon your deeds," he said to one and all
And he reiterated that all usury was forthwith banned
Beginning with the usury that was due to his clan

The old blood ways were henceforth abolished
The hearts of the people he wanted to polish
And the distortion of time was that day erased
To bring to the people the Lord's Loving Grace

NOBLE BROTHER

Men and women have obligations and rights
Different but equal are they in the Lord's Sight
Worship the Lord thy God with all sincerity
Pray, fast, go to the House, and give charity

All of the people are from Adam and Eve
No one is superior except by God's leave
You are not best by your skin or family line
But by how close your actions follow the Divine

"O People," he told all those standing in the valley
"No Prophet or Messenger will come after me."
So he told the people to stay true to the Lord's way
So that they will see bliss on Judgment Day

Two things he left for the people to obey
God's Holy Book and the Prophet's Noble Way
And if they stay true to these blessed things
The pain of sin will neither burn nor sting

And as he finished his talk, he asked once more
If he had faithfully sent the message he bore
And as they said "Yes," his speech came to an end
And many of them would never see their friend again

His Work is Done

NOBLE BROTHER

His work is done, and the people have believed
The disquiet in the soul he has beautifully relieved
Order was restored to the House Abraham built
Out of scattered tribes was sewn a radiant quilt

The darkness of the past was put to dust
A Shine on the hearts replaced the ugly rust
A new era of humanity was beautifully conceived
When his work was done, and the people did believe

The pains of death began to slowly creep
And the faithful started to silently weep
Must it be that the Messenger would now soon leave?
For his work was done, and the people have believed?

Weakness began to overtake his body
So much that he could not pray communally
Men and women would soon be bereaved
For his work was done, and the people have believed

Who could lead, once the Prophet is gone?
Who could guide our precious young and fawn?
What will we do when Revelation will cease?
And faith will wane, and knowledge will decrease?

A more urgent matter: the Prophet is too weak
He cannot pray and the Companions now seek
Someone to lead in ritual adoration
So the Prophet chose to his adulation

And as he laid in his home, he opened and beheld
The believers in prayer standing as one and meld
A smile came to his face, and he was greatly relieved
For his work was done, and the people have believed

Then came the choice from the Lord on High
Whether to stay with us or to say goodbye
The response was clear, and he needed no advice
He chose his Lord and the bliss of Paradise

In the lap of his beloved, did his soul finally depart
And she screamed in agony, for she now had to part
With the love of her life, who graced one and all
With wisdom and light to help avoid the fall

Darkness filled the land, although Sun was bright
White became black, day turned into night
No one ever thought that he could ever leave
But his work was done, and the people have believed

PART TWO: THE EPIC OF HIS CHARACTER

HESHAM A. HASSABALLA

A declaration of the Beloved on High
For eternity is this truth inscribed
That as the end of our days is neigh
A Messenger of great character described

From the days of childhood did he shine
Actions always worthy of praise
Guided by his Precious Lord, the Divine
Few were not warmed by his rays

With little to hold in hand did he grow
Because of holy and generous pledge
To feed and water the pilgrims' flow
He would thus walk to hunger's edge

When food would grace his uncle's table
He would hold back with utter humility
He would not eat, though he was surely able
And he would go hungry with regular stability

Father's brother finally took a keen eye
And he realized that his favorite son withheld
And so he would stop them, despite their cry
To feed the one whose magnificence he beheld

A time honored journey was now his to tread
In the employ of a most honorable dame
She sent him and her servant to transact in her stead
To see if he would prosper or be worthy of blame

"Never did I see such an honorable man!
Who was always kind, though I am only slave
His nobility shined through his mercantile plan
And he was neither a charlatan nor a knave!

NOBLE BROTHER

Yet there was something even greater than this:
Something which I had not heretofore seen
A cloud would follow to shade and give bliss
So that the Sun could not harm or demean

And when he sat to gain rest under a tree
Scribe and scholar came out to declare
With complete faith and an amazing decree
That none but a Prophet sits alone over there!

And so I went back to tell all to my Lady
About the magnificence of this man
Her eyes widened at his incredible beauty
And therewith was hatched a most noble plan!"

Time has passed, and the Lord has declared
That His House must now be forever cleaned
So Messenger preached, and teeth became bared
From father's brother, who wretchedly demeaned

Whenever the Prophet would preach the Lord's word
His Blood would follow to discredit and malign:
"Don't pay heed to the things you just heard!
A wretched man is this young nephew of mine!"

But the Messenger did not fight or even restrain
An uncle whose character was dark as night
Continue, he did, to make God's Word most plain
And he left his uncle to stain him in plain sight

Day after day, the filth lies in wait
For the Messenger to walk in its path
Yet, he does nothing to this act ingrate
Neither does he avenge or even show wrath

Yet the message grows, and the enemy is brutal
It attacks and kills those who follow the Elect
With the Messenger they spare no evil withal
Try to attack and even kill they do not neglect

Yet Mecca is a City with many an evil soul
Hard, it was, to find someone magnanimous
To protect their wealth, they give to control
All to Muhammad, though they make his life perilous

When the Emissary can no longer take any more
He travels to a place in order to find an ally
Yet there he finds a host with ugliness in store
And with his noble call they brutally fail to comply

Yet leave him alone they dare do not
Evil is the plan that their minds do hone
After him, they sent, in the Sun so hot
Urchin and thug to expel him with stone

And as he lay under shade from heat
Soldiers of God do powerfully descend
They deny that he was handed defeat
With the mountainside, him they will defend

But the Messenger says to leave them be
He refuses to crush under their wrath
The Emissary shows true magnanimity
Hoping the city in time follows God's path

Yet Mecca has failed to grasp His light
Insolent in refusal she continues to be
And so to the North believers take flight
Where they can at long last live and be free

NOBLE BROTHER

Yet one does not leave, as all others flee
Remain behind, despite threat to his life
He returns enemy's goods in full honesty
Showing grace to those who showed him strife

At last he arrives in the City of Light
With total glee do his followers rejoice
Safe and secure after many days of flight
And he enjoins thus in his glorious voice:

"Spread peace," he begins his talk
"Feed the hungry" he continues in glory
"Pray when others sleep" is God's path to walk
On the way to Paradise in peace and glory.

Wave after wave of hatred and guile
Besiege the believers in their City of Light
Repel their swords he does all the while
Defending his flock with his glorious might

At foot of Mount the enemies meet to spar
A clear command disobeyed without grace
Enemies descend upon the Prophet from afar
And nearly kill him as he stood in his place

Then he sat on Mount, all bloodied and weak
Companions sear in pain from terrible folly
Neither revenge nor punishment did he seek
For breach of command that hurt him dearly

Yet tides turn and the City in strength gains
Enemies make a truce, and faith fills the land
But to this pact, the enemy shows its disdain
And the Prophet marches with victory at hand

There he stands, with Holy House in full view
And he asks vicious enemy about previous deed:
"What do you think I will do to you?"
But as they cower, he sets them free with speed

Another victory graces the Emissary's band
And victim released makes feast for glee
Yet guile and murder stood behind her hand
For she sought to poison him and quickly flee

But the Lord is on his side, and plot was found
He confronts the woman who sought to kill
He sets her free for his grace and mercy abound
And shows the world that God's mercy is great still

Ink would dry and parchment would cease
Before the full story of his grace is told
I pray thee to learn and thy knowledge increase
Of the Noble Brother and how his grace unfolds!

APPENDIX

Brutality and a New Dawn

The time preceding the advent of the Prophet
Muhammad was one of brutality and hatred.
Tribalism reigned supreme, and tribes would fight to
the death to defend one of their own, even if he be
guilty of a crime. People were enslaved by usurious
practices, and there was nothing to stop the strong
and politically powerful from preying on the weak
and helpless.

In the city of Mecca, the birthplace of the Prophet,
the tribe of Quraysh was dominant. It dictated the
terms of the annual Pilgrimage, a vestige of the
ancient monotheistic faith of the Patriarch Abraham,
and the Arabs had to comply. This, along with its role
in hosting and taking care of the pilgrims, was the
source of Quraysh's tremendous wealth and
influence. It was also, however, the source of its
corruption, especially when it came to religious
practices. For instance, pilgrims could only venerate
the Ka'bah – the central shrine in Mecca built by
Abraham for the worship of the One God – with
clothes purchased from Quraysh. If they did not have
the means to do so, they were forced to walk around
the Ka'bah totally naked.

There were many religions practiced in the Arabian
Peninsula at the time of the birth of the Prophet
Muhammad. These included Christianity, Judaism,
and a form of Abrahamic Unitarianism. The
dominant religion, however, was idolatry. At the time
of the Prophet's birth, the Ka'bah had been overtaken
by over 360 idols, representing the gods of the

various Arab tribes.

As he would come to learn many years later, the
mission of the Prophet Muhammad was to restore the
worship of the One God of Abraham to its rightful
place. Moreover, the Prophet was also tasked to turn
this brutal environment into one of justice, equality,
and noble character.

Year of the Elephant

The pre-Islamic Arabs did not have an established calendar system by which they kept track of the passage of time. Whenever significant events would occur, they would name that particular year after that particular event. The year in which the Prophet Muhammad was born was such a year: the Year of the Elephant.

There was a dispute in Yemen, the southernmost part of the Arabian Peninsula, between various factions of its Abyssinian masters. In order to show his loyalty to the Negus, or King of Abyssinia, the ruler of Yemen, Abraha, built a very large cathedral and wanted the Arabs to venerate this church instead of the Ka'bah. The Arabs, for their part, refused to comply. In fact, a Bedouin made that very point extremely clear by desecrating the walls of the church with his own feces. This act of defiance enraged Abraha to such an extent that he raised an army, with elephants at its helm, to destroy the Ka'bah.

This army, including Abraha, was destroyed by an enormous flock of tiny birds, each carrying three small pebbles. The Qur'an (Chapter 105) recounts this story:

Art thou not aware of how thy Lord dealt with the Army of the Elephant? Did He not utterly confound their artful planning? And let loose upon them great swarms of flying creatures, which smote them with stone-hard blows of chastisement pre-ordained, and caused them to become like a field of grain that has been eaten down to stubble?

A Sacred Union

This poem recounts the story of the marriage of the Prophet's father Abd-Allah, to his mother Aminah, the daughter of Wahb. His mother was from the city of Yathrib, north of Mecca. Soon after their marriage, the Prophet Muhammad was born, but not before his father passed away.

On the day of his birth, the Jewish tribes of Yathrib hailed the coming of "Ahmad," the awaited Prophet, and his grandfather – Abd Al Mutalib – was most pleased with this new grandson.

They Passed Him By

It was customary among the city-dwellers of Mecca to send their children to be reared and nursed by the Bedouins of the desert. They felt that the desert upbringing was tremendously beneficial, giving the child proper mastery of the Arabic language and an austerity that was lacking in city life. The Prophet's mother followed in this tradition.

When the wet-nurses, however, came to claim the children, they all passed up the Prophet Muhammad, seeing that he was an orphan. A woman named Halimah, of the tribe of Bani Sa'ad, had initially passed on the Prophet, but she changed her mind as she did not want to leave Mecca without any child to nurse.

This proved to be the best decision she had ever made. The young Prophet brought nothing but blessing and plenty to she and her family. In fact, her mule – weak and feeble on its way to Mecca – returned to Bani Sa'ad with a strength beyond its years, to the amazement of all in her tribe. Her land and sheep, long since barren, began to bear fruit and milk, again to the amazement of all in her tribe. When the time came for Halimah to return the Prophet to his mother, Halimah begged her to keep him with her, for she did not want the blessings to cease.

The Boy and the Monk

When the Prophet Muhammad was around eleven years old, he was living with his uncle Abu Talib, after both his mother and grandfather had died. Every year, the Meccans would travel to Syria for business, and one day, the young Prophet begged his uncle to accompany him on one of these trips.

On the way, the caravan stopped by a monastery which housed a monk, and contrary to all other times, the monk showed great interest in the young Prophet. He asked the Prophet a question in the name of "*al lat and al uzza*," the names of two of their goddesses, as was customary among the pagan Arabs. The Prophet took strong objection to this question, which greatly surprised the monk. He then looked at his back and found a birthmark which every Prophet bore, called the "Seal of Prophethood."

The monk knew immediately that this boy was the awaited Prophet foretold in Scripture, and he went to Abu Talib and asked: "How is this boy related to you?" Abu Talib answered: "He is my son," to which the monk answered: "It is impossible that this boy's father is alive!" Abu Talib then confirmed: "He is my brother's son." The monk bade Abu Talib to send the Prophet back to Mecca for, if he was discovered, he was liable to be killed. Abu Talib complied.

He Came to Town One Day

In Arabia, there were men who possessed a knowledge called *Al Firasah*, which was an ability to foretell someone's future by observing their facial features. One such man came to Mecca one day, and Abu Talib took the young Prophet to see him.

When the man beheld the Prophet, he stared at him with such an intensity that it frightened Abu Talib, and he sent the Prophet back home. The man did not notice this for he became distracted, but when he realized that the Prophet had gone home, he screamed out asking for the Prophet to come back. He also said, "By God! This boy will have a grand future!" This left Abu Talib most pleased.

Noble Brother

This poem recounts the story of Um Mu'bad, a Bedouin woman who recounted the most accurate and famous description of the Prophet Muhammad's physical features. Most of the biographies of the Prophet include her story, which occurred much later in his life, during his flight from Mecca to Yathrib.

The Prophet and Abu Bakr, his long-time friend and companion, stopped by the home of Um Mu'bad and asked if she had anything to drink. Due to her poverty, she had to refuse him saying, "Had we had anything to give, you would not need to ask."

The Prophet then asked if she had any animals which they could milk. She replied that she only had one animal, which had long since been barren. Miraculously, he milked the animal, and the Prophet, Abu Bakr, and Um Mu'bad all drank to their fill. In addition, he filled all of their vessels with this milk, to the wonderment of Um Mu'bad.

After the Prophet left, her husband – who was away at the time of the Prophet's visit – asked about this newly filled milk, and she replied: "A truly blessed man has just passed by us!"

The Honest One

The Prophet Muhammad's honesty was beyond reproach, and his name was *Al Amin*, or "The Honest One," among Quraysh. In fact, one of his most bitter enemies – Abu Jahl – remarked: "O Muhammad! I do not say that you are a liar! I only deny what you brought and that to which you call the people." In addition, his upbringing was free of the licentiousness that was common among the young Arab men of the Prophet's time. Tradition recounts that whenever the Prophet would consider doing something unclean, he would fall asleep.

When the Prophet was coming into his own as a young man, the Quraysh decided to rebuild the Ka'bah. When it came time to place the sacred Black Stone in the corner, a dispute ensued over which tribe would have the honor to place it there. This almost led to bloodshed, and a wise man said, "Let the next man who enters this gate mediate your dispute." That man turned out to be the Prophet Muhammad, to which they all remarked enthusiastically: "The 'Honest One'? We all agree!" The Prophet's wise solution to this dispute averted a major tribal war.

A Love Story

This poem recounts how the Prophet Muhammad came to marry his first and most beloved wife, Khadijah, the daughter of Khuwaylid. She was a very wealthy businesswoman, who was a widow and had lost interest in marrying again. She took the Prophet Muhammad into her employ because of his impeccable reputation for honesty and integrity.

His skill as a merchant, along with his incredible character, deeply impressed her, and the embers of love were kindled in her heart once more. She proposed marriage to the Prophet, who accepted. At the time of their union, he was twenty-five, and she was forty. She bore him six children, and it was a very happy and successful marriage. The Prophet never stopped loving Khadijah his entire life.

Retreat to the Cave

As the Prophet approached the age of forty, he became increasingly disturbed by the rampant injustice of his day, and the worship of idols deeply bothered him as well. These things led him to retreat to the cave of Hira, not far outside of Mecca, to meditate for various periods of time, especially during the month of Ramadan. A great event occurred on one of these spiritual retreats.

Once Upon A Powerful Night

This poem recounts the Night of Power, during which the Prophet was commissioned by God and the Qur'an was first revealed. As the Prophet was meditating in the cave of Hira, he was suddenly made aware of a presence that filled the entire cave, heretofore dark, with light. The presence approached the Prophet and commanded him thus: "Read!"

"I cannot read," was the Prophet's reply.

The Presence then squeezed the Prophet so tightly that he thought he was going to die, after which the Presence repeated: "Read!"

"I cannot read," repeated a terrified Prophet.

The Presence then squeezed him yet again so tightly that the Prophet thought he was going to die, and after he was released, the Presence said yet again: "Read!"

"I cannot read," the Prophet said once more, but the Presence squeezed him again. The Prophet then said, "What shall I read?"

The Angel then said:

Read in the name of thy Lord who created. Created man from something which clings. Read, and your Lord is most noble. He taught by the pen. He taught humanity that which it did not know.

The Angel then vanished, leaving the Prophet in sheer terror. When the Prophet left the cave, the Angel reappeared, now straddling the horizon, and declared: "O Muhammad! You are the Messenger of God, and I am Gabriel." Every where the Prophet looked, he saw the Angel there. After a while, the Angel vanished.

The words revealed to him were the first five verse of chapter ninety-six of the Qur'an. This event, commemorated every year in the month of Ramadan, marked a new era in human history: the advent of Islam and the ministry of the long-awaited Last Prophet, Muhammad, the son of Abd-Allah.

"Cover Me!"

After the tremendous and terrifying experience of the First Revelation, the Prophet rushed home to his beloved Khadijah, trembling from fear. This frightened her greatly, and after the Prophet's fear subsided, he recounted to her the story.

He confided that he feared he was afflicted by an evil spirit, to which she replied: "You are kind to relatives, you speak only the truth, you help the poor, and orphan, and the needy. God will never let you down." She then took her husband to her cousin, Waraqah, who was a Christian and Biblical scholar. The Prophet told him the story, and Waraqah was astonished, confirming that he was indeed the Prophet of his people.

First Call

After a short while, the Prophet was commanded to call his people to the way of the One God. One morning, he climbed on top of a small mount and called out to his people. They answered his call, and when they gathered unto him, he said:

"O my people! If I told you that, behind this hill, was an army about to attack you, would you believe me?"

They all replied in the affirmative. The Prophet then warned them of an impending punishment if they do not worship the One God. In the middle of his speech, his own uncle Abu Lahab screamed out: "May you perish! Is this the thing for which you brought us here?" He then dispersed the people, preventing the Prophet from finishing his talk. This event marked the beginning of the struggle to bring the message of Islam to the people of Mecca, and it showed how tenacious the opposition to his call – just as Waraqah had predicted – will be.

Flight to the King

As the message of Islam began to grow, so did Quraysh's violent opposition and suppression. Although the Prophet himself was well protected by his clan, Bani Hashim, many of his followers did not enjoy the same level of protection. They were brutally tortured, and some were even killed. Under the pressure of this brutality, the Prophet urged a number of his followers – including members of his own family – to flee to Abyssinia, where a just Christian king ruled and would give them shelter.

The Quraysh learned of this, and they sent emissaries to retrieve these "religious rebels," as they called them, from the king. When the Muslims recounted to the king the story of the birth of Jesus Christ in the Qur'an, he was deeply moved and gave the Muslims refuge in his land for as long as they desired. In fact, the king later accepted Islam, keeping his faith a secret until his death.

The Hunter Submits

One day in Mecca, as the Prophet was circumambulating the Ka'bah, he was verbally assaulted by one of his worst enemies: Amr, the son of Hisham, or Abu Jahl, or "Father of Ignorance," as the Muslims called him. Although greatly vexed by the insults, the Prophet did not answer him and left. When his uncle, Hamza, learned of this incident, he became enraged and rushed to Abu Jahl, striking him with his bow in revenge. He then said, "Do you attack him when I follow his faith, saying exactly what he says?"

Although he said it in anger, he later came to accept Islam and declared his faith to his overjoyed nephew. From that day forward, Hamza was a steadfast supporter of Islam and defender of the Prophet Muhammad. His conversion gave the nascent faith a great boost of strength and influence.

"Today I Am Going To Kill This Man!"

These were the words of Umar, the son of Al Khattab, one of the staunchest enemies of Islam, on the morning that he accepted Islam. He was determined to kill the Prophet and end the communal divide that Islam had caused. On his way to the Prophet's house, a Muslim (whose faith was a secret) noticed that Umar was up to something serious and inquired about his intention.

Umar declared his decision to kill the Prophet Muhammad, and seeing the seriousness on his face, the Muslim feared for the Prophet's life. Thus, he revealed to Umar that Fatimah, Umar's sister, had also become a Muslim, which enraged him. The Muslim did this to buy time in order to warn the Prophet.

As the Prophet was being warned, Umar set straightaway for his sister's house. When she confirmed her faith, he struck her violently, drawing blood. Seeing his sister on the ground bleeding softened his heart, however, and he asked to read a part of the Qur'an he had heard being recited as he came to her door.

After reading them – the first passage of chapter twenty – he was deeply affected, and he asked to go see the Prophet. He went to the house at which the Prophet was staying, sword still in hand, and knocked on the door. The Muslims inside – save Hamza and the Prophet – were scared: they had been warned of Umar's intentions. When Umar entered into the

Prophet's presence, he fell to his knees and made the declaration of faith. His conversion was an enormous victory for the Muslims, and it shook Quraysh to the core. Now, the Muslims had another important and powerful ally, the mighty Umar son of Al Khattab. In fact, after Umar's conversion, the Muslims stopped worshiping and meeting in secret.

Enemy's Plan

Quraysh did not fail to come up with even more brutal and vicious ways to suffocate the new faith. This time, they decided to boycott and starve the Prophet and his followers, clan, and family. For three years, they banished the Prophet to the hills outside Mecca and placed upon them a harsh regime of social and economic sanctions.

The Prophet and his followers, consequently, suffered greatly from this boycott: it directly led to the deaths of both his uncle Abu Talib, his main protector and supporter, and Khadijah, his beloved wife, companion, and mother of his children. Over time, however, many members of Quraysh decried the boycott, and they broke the sanctions against the Prophet.

In fact, when the boycott was first imposed, a parchment was drafted outlining its terms and it was nailed to the door of the Ka'bah. When they sought to tear it down, the parchment had been eaten by tiny insects, and all that was left was a piece that contained the words: "In Your Name, O God."

Year of Sadness/Second City

The year that brought about the death of Abu Talib and Khadijah was the darkest moment in the Prophet's life and ministry. Due to the horrific and brutal opposition in Mecca, the Prophet hoped to gain some support from the people of Ta'if, the "Second City," which housed the tribe of Bani Thaqif.

Initially, he was warmly greeted by their leaders. When the learned of his message, however, they rejected him immediately. The Prophet then asked to be allowed to preach Islam to their people. The leaders not only refused, but sent children and street urchins to stone the Prophet's feet until they were bloodied, driving him out of the city.

After his expulsion from Ta'if, it was so dangerous for the Prophet – now that Abu Talib was dead – that he could not re-enter Mecca without protection. The Prophet thought all was lost, but the Lord had something very significant in store for His Noble Messenger.

Arise, O Gallant Son

Given the difficult situation of the Muslims in Mecca, the Prophet feared he was doing something wrong. Perhaps he was making God angry? The Lord, however, was not angry with him, and to show this to the Prophet, God took him from Mecca to Jerusalem, where he ascended to Heaven, in one night. This famous journey is called the *Isra' wal Mi'raj*, or "The Transport and Ascension," and it is recounted in the Qur'an:

Limitless in His glory is He who transported His servant by night from the Inviolable House of Worship [at Mecca] to the Remote House of Worship [at Jerusalem] - the environs of which We had blessed - so that We might show him some of Our symbols: for, verily, He alone is all-hearing, all-seeing. (17:1)

When he arrived in Jerusalem, he led all of the Prophets in prayer. He then ascended to Heaven and saw things that no other Prophet had seen. The culmination of his ascent was his entrance into the Divine Presence, where he talked to God directly.

This amazing journey confirmed to the Prophet that God had not forsaken him, and the opposition of Quraysh was part of God's plan. The next day, the Prophet recounted what had happened to him, to his great ridicule. It was a major test of faith for the Muslims, and some Muslims, in fact, left Islam in sheer shock over this truly unbelievable story.

The Quraysh asked him to describe Jerusalem to them, and he did so perfectly, to their great amazement, for they all knew the Prophet never set foot in Jerusalem before. Moreover, the Prophet told them about a caravan that was coming three days hence and gave specific descriptions about it. His words came true exactly.

The Pledge

When it seemed that all hope was lost for the mission
of the Prophet, a small delegation from the city of
Yathrib, some 250 miles north of Mecca, accepted
Islam and beseeched the Prophet to come to their
city. He accepted their pledge of loyalty, and he then
commanded the believers to emigrate to Yathrib and
leave Mecca behind. This event, called the *Hijrah*, or
"Migration," marks the beginning of the Islamic
calendar. Yathrib later became known as *Medinat-un-
Nabi Al Munawwarah*, or "The Enlightened City of the
Prophet." It has since been known as simply
Medinah.

HESHAM A. HASSABALLA

Joyous Welcome

After all the believers who were able to emigrate to
Medinah did so safely, the Prophet and Abu Bakr
finally made the journey to the North. Awaiting them
was an eager and joyous community of believers,
which greeted the Prophet with song and poetry.

Before he left, however, the Meccans plotted to
assassinate the Prophet and had actually stood outside
the door to his house waiting for him to leave. Their
plans failed, and the Prophet walked right past them
without they even noticing he was there. He was
reciting this verse of chapter 36:

*We have set a barrier before them and a barrier behind them,
and We have enshrouded them in veils so that they cannot see.*

Enemies Make War

The Quraysh was incensed that the Prophet was able to escape their clutches and flee to Medinah. This new kingdom, as it were, was a threat to their religious and economic hegemony. Thus, they declared open war upon the Muslim community in Yathrib.

First, they confiscated all of the belongings that the Muslims left behind and lined their caravans with them. In retaliation, the Prophet raided as many of the caravans of Quraysh as he could. This led to the first major battle between Mecca and Medinah: the Battle of Badr.

During this battle, 300 or so poorly equipped Muslims faced a well-armed Meccan force of 1,000. In a matter of hours, the Meccan army was routed, shaking the entire Arabian Peninsula. Most of the leaders of Quraysh were killed at Badr, and it was an enormous victory for the Muslims.

Brutal Vengeance

In shock at their stunning defeat, the Meccans' fury grew ever stronger, and they sent an even larger force – three thousand – to Medinah to finish off the nascent Muslim community. Although the Prophet expressed a desire to stay within the confines of the naturally fortified Medinah, his followers' urged him to meet the enemy head on, and he complied. The armies met once again at the foot of Mount Uhud, not far outside of Medinah.

The battle began with another decisive Muslim victory at hand, but a group of archers which the Prophet strategically placed between the two camps disobeyed his orders to stay in their places. The majority of the archers, thinking the battle was over and eager to share in the booty, left their small hill unguarded. Khalid, the son of Al Walid, noticed this and took immediate advantage, charging upon the Muslims and attacking them by surprise.

Chaos ensured, and the Prophet himself was nearly killed. He was struck hard and fell into a trap, and many Muslims actually believed him to be dead. Yet, the Prophet and the Muslims were able to escape to the Mount of Uhud, and the battle ended in a stalemate. Still, the Meccans took further revenge and mutilated the bodies of the fallen Muslim warriors, including the body of Hamza, the Prophet's uncle.

Final Blow

Since the previous battle of Uhud really did not achieve any of the Meccans' strategic objectives – and in many respects was actually a victory for the Prophet – the Meccans devised another plan of attack. They gathered as many of the Arab tribes as they could into an unprecedented force and marched on the city of Medinah itself. Their army numbered 10,000 men, and the Prophet decided to stay within the city to defend it.

Moreover, the Prophet took a page out of the playbook of the Persians, digging trenches around the entrances to the city, confounding the Meccan army. A siege of over thirty days ensued, and it was a dire situation for the Muslim camp, as a large group of Hypocrites – outward Muslims but really enemies bent on destroying Islam from within – abandoned the Muslim army. Furthermore, the tribe of Bani Qurayza, heretofore allied with the Muslims, broke their treaty and colluded with the Meccan army to attack from behind.

At this most dangerous moment, a man by the name of Nu'aym, the son of Mas'ud, converted to Islam and defected to the Prophet's camp and offered his services. The Prophet told him to break this evil alliance by any means he could, and through a brilliant ruse, the alliance between Mecca and Bani Qurayza was foiled.

Soon thereafter, a fierce and cold wild relentlessly afflicted both camps, and the Meccans lost heart and withdrew their forces from the city. The Battle of the Trench, as it had come to be known, marked the last major battle between Mecca and Medinah, and henceforth, the Meccans never attacked the Muslims in a formal fashion again.

Pilgrimage

After the Battle of the Trench, the Prophet had a dream that he and his Companions were making a lesser pilgrimage in Mecca. He thus announced his intention to make such a pilgrimage to Mecca with his followers, a surprising move as the state of war with Mecca had not abated in the least.

The Prophet encamped just outside the sacred boundary of the Precincts, where no one can be injured or hurt, and this confused the Meccans as to his intentions. The Prophet maintained that he only wished to make a lesser pilgrimage, but the Meccans refused his entry out of guile, ruining their images because Arab custom dictated that no one – not even your most brutal enemy – can be barred from visiting the Holy House.

Negotiations ensued, and they culminated in the Treaty of Hudaybiyah. The agreement stipulated that the Muslims must return to Medinah this year, but they can return next year for three days to make a lesser pilgrimage. A ten year truce would commence, and no one would harm the other. In addition, any Muslim defecting from Mecca had to be returned to Mecca, but any Muslim defecting from Medinah could stay with the Meccans.

Furthermore, the Treaty would be binding upon any tribe that wished to ally itself with either side. At that moment, the tribe of Khuza'ah declared its alliance with the Prophet, and the tribe of Bani Bakr declared it alliance with Quraysh.

On the surface, the Treaty seemed to humiliate the Prophet, and it caused much consternation and disappointment in the Muslim camp. Even Umar, one of the Prophet's closest companions, rebuked the Prophet harshly for his agreeing to this pact. The Prophet, however, was assured by God that this Treaty would be in the Muslims' favor.

Less than two years later, the promise of God – embodied in this verse: *We have indeed given thee a manifest victory* (48:1) – was indeed fulfilled.

Vile Betrayal

The Meccans never intended to keep to the terms of
the Treaty of Hudaybiyah, and they used that time to
gather their strength for a renewed attack on the
Prophet. Yet, they went a step further and aided a
surprise attack on the tribe of Khuza'ah – allies of the
Prophet – by the tribe of Bani Bakr. Worse still, this
attack occurred within the Sacred Precinct, making it
a act of vile treachery. It was a clear breach of the
Treaty of Hudaybiyah.

Although Mecca tried to conceal her actions, word of
the treachery reached the ears of an incensed Prophet
Muhammad, and he immediately gathered a force of
10,000 men and marched upon Mecca in retribution
and defense of his ally. The advance of the Prophet
upon Mecca was unstoppable, and he conquered the
city with hardly a drop of bloodshed. At the pinnacle
of his victory, he entered the city with his head bowed
in utter humility before God.

Then, after centuries of their veneration at the
Ka'bah, all of the idols were destroyed before the
Meccans' eyes. The idolatry that defiled the House of
God that Abraham built was once and for all
destroyed. After this, most of Mecca accepted Islam
and became part of the Muslim community.

Final Admonition

The remaining pockets of hostile resistance have been defeated, and nearly the entire Arabian Peninsula accepted Islam. Now, the Prophet returns to Mecca to make his *Hajj*, or once-in-a-lifetime greater pilgrimage to Mecca.

After completing the rites of the *Hajj*, he gave his famous final sermon, where he advised the Muslims about their conduct and actions. He finally abolished the practice of usury, and he declared racial and ethnic superiority null and void. He affirmed the equality of men and women before God. He wiped away the old tribal customs and encouraged the believers to come together in brotherhood.

He repeatedly asked his followers to bear witness that he has delivered the message, to which they all bore witness, for, as he himself said, "I know not whether after this year, I shall ever be amongst you again."

His Work is Done

The ministry of the Prophet Muhammad has now come to a close. He soon fell ill, and this illness proved to be his last. He died in the lap of his beloved wife A'isha, the daughter of his beloved companion Abu Bakr, in Medinah in 632 A.D.

It came as a total shock to the Muslim community. The Muslims could not believe that the man they loved, their direct link to the Divine, had passed away. In fact, Umar refused to believe that the Prophet had died, threatening to kill anyone who maintained that the Prophet was dead.

It was Abu Bakr who climbed upon the Prophet's pulpit and put such actions to rest:

"Whoever of you worshipped Muhammad, know that Muhammad has died. Whoever of you worshipped God, know that He is alive and never dies."

Then Abu Bakr recited this verse of the Qur'an:

Muhammad is only an apostle; all the [other] apostles have passed away before him: if, then, he dies or is slain, will you turn about on your heels? But he that turns about on his heels can in no wise harm God - whereas God will requite all who are grateful [to Him] (3:144)

The Epic of His Character

This epic tells some of the tales of the Prophet's magnanimous and magnificent character.

When he was a young boy, living in the house of Abu Talib, he would never rush and eat the food as his cousins would do. Thus, on many an evening, he would sleep hungry. His uncle Abu Talib finally noticed this, and he stopped all others from eating until the Prophet himself would eat.

When Khadijah sent the Prophet to conduct business on her behalf, she sent with him her servant Maysarah. After the trip, she asked him about the Prophet, and Maysarah recounted how truly amazing his character was; how there was a cloud that constantly followed them as they journeyed in the desert; how a monk told Maysarah: "None other but a Prophet sits under that tree."

After the Prophet Muhammad was commissioned to spread the message of Islam to his people, his uncle Abu Lahab declared open hostility to him. In fact, so hostile was Abu Lahab, that he would follow the Prophet throughout Mecca and tell those to whom the Prophet had just spoken to disregard everything the Prophet has said to them. Never did the Prophet stop him.

Every day, the Prophet would find filth and garbage at his front door, yet he would never strike back in revenge or anger. In fact, tradition states that once, when he found no garbage at his front door, he learned that the person who would place said garbage at his front door was sick. He subsequently visited her to make sure she was doing well. This touched the woman deeply.

The viciousness of the Meccans knew no bounds, and they frequently attacked both the Prophet and his followers. Yet, the only person with whom these selfsame enemies entrusted their valuables was none other than the Prophet himself. In fact, he delayed his own migration to Yathrib, in part, to return these valuables to these enemies.

After the Prophet Muhammad was expelled from Ta'if in a most ugly manner – stoned by thug and street urchin – he was visited by Gabriel and two Angels. The Archangel told the Prophet that, with his command, his two angelic companions would crush Ta'if under the mountains that surround it. The Prophet, however, refused such vengeance. He said that he hoped their children would one day become believers, a hope which was fulfilled in his own lifetime.

Soon after the Prophet arrives in Yathrib, now called Medinah, he tells his followers:

Spread peace; feed the hungry; keep the family ties; pray when others are sleeping, and you will enter Paradise safe and secure.

This prophetic advice was so grand in its eloquence that I could not help but enshrine it in verse.

Battle after battle was waged in defense of the Muslim

community in Medinah. After the defeat of the pagans at Badr, they marched again on Medinah and met the Muslims at Uhud. Despite his nearly being killed as a result of the disobedience of the Archers, the Prophet took no revenge against them. The Qur'an confirms this stance:

And it was by God's grace that thou [O Prophet] didst deal gently with thy followers: for if thou hadst been harsh and hard of heart, they would indeed have broken away from thee. (3:159)

Despite all the efforts at destroying the Islamic project, the enemies of the Prophet failed, and he marched victorious into Mecca as conqueror. With dread upon all of their faces, the Prophet asked his vicious and brutal enemies, "What do you think I will do with you?" They all replied: "You are a Noble Brother, son of a Noble Brother." He then said, "I will take no revenge upon you. Go, for you are free."

Another great victory was the one granted to the Prophet at Khaybar, a region to the north of Medinah. After the battle, a woman prepared a feast of poisoned meat for the Prophet, to avenge the defeat of her people. The Prophet took a small bite, but he was miraculously advised that the meat was poisoned. When the woman was summoned to answer for what she did, the Prophet did not take revenge against her and let her go.

These are just some of the amazing stories of the Prophet's truly remarkable character, and it is as I had written before:

NOBLE BROTHER

Ink would dry and parchment would cease
Before the full story of his grace is told
I pray thee to learn and thy knowledge increase
Of the Noble Brother and how his grace unfolds!

Your Shoulder

NOBLE BROTHER

They laughed and jeered because you I followed
They joked and sneered and many times I wallowed
In the loneliness that comes with walking your way
And staying forever true to what you say

And I needed your shoulder, for me to cry on
The softness of your lap, for me to lie on
If I could have reached out and held your hand
It would have been easier for me to stand

Day in and day out, they call you ruthless
Blood-thirsty and mean, a man most godless
It pains my heart to hear you so called
And what they say makes me so appalled

And I could use your shoulder, for me to cry on
The softness of your lap, for me to lie one
If I could reach out and hold your hand
It would make it easier for me to stand

They look at her and scream out in a state
Of anger and scorn, with guile and hate
No crimes did she commit, no law did she break
Save put a scarf on her head for modesty's sake

And she could use your shoulder, for her to cry on
The softness of your lap, for her to lie on
If she could reach out and hold your hand
It would make it easier for her to stand

But alas, Master, your shoulder we cannot have
Your soft, sweet hand has long gone away
You were taken away, my precious man
To the King On High, So Glorious all along

And though we all yearn so much for you now
We know that with Him, we will make it somehow.

I know that there will be more hills to climb
And I could use your presence, so sublime
But since you left me with a hand Divine
I will not go wrong; I will be just fine.

SUGGESTED READINGS

Hassaballa, Hesham A and Helminski, Kabir. *The Beliefnet Guide to Islam.* New York: Three Leaves Press, 2006.

Armstrong, Karen. *Islam: A Short History.* New York: Modern Library, 2002.

Lings, Martin. *Muhammad: His Life Based on the Earliest Sources.* Rochester, VT: Inner Traditions, 1987.

Asad , Muhammad. *The Message of the Qur'an.* Bristol, UK: The Book Foundation, 2003.

Yusuf, Hamza (translator), and Mazrui Al-Amin Ali (collector). *The Content of Character: Ethical Sayings of the Prophet Muhammad.* Cambridge, UK: Sandala, 2005.

ABOUT THE AUTHOR

Hesham A. Hassaballa is a Chicago doctor and writer. He has written extensively on a freelance basis, being published in newspapers across the country and around the world. He has been a Beliefnet columnist since 2001, and has written for the Religion News Service. He is also a columnist for Patheos.

His articles have been distributed worldwide by Agence Global, and he was also a guest blogger for The Chicago Tribune before joining ChicagoNow, where he currently blogs. In addition, Dr. Hassaballa has appeared as a guest on WTTW (Channel 11) in Chicago, CNN, Fox News, BBC, and National Public Radio.

Dr. Hassaballa is co-author of The Beliefnet Guide to Islam (Doubleday), and his essay, "Why I Love the Ten Commandments," was published in the award-winning book Taking Back Islam (Rodale). His forthcoming work of fiction, Code Blue, will be published by Faithful Word Press.

In 2007, his blog "God, Faith, and a Pen" was nominated for a Brass Crescent Award for a blog that is "the most stimulating, insightful, and philosophical, providing the best rebuttals to extremist ideology and making an impact whenever they post."

In addition to writing, Dr. Hassaballa helped found the Chicago Chapter of the Council on American Islamic Relations and currently serves on their board of directors. He also co-founded the Bayan H. Hassaballa Charitable Foundation and serves as its Executive Director.

www.ingramcontent.com/pod-product-compliance
Lightning Source LLC
Chambersburg PA
CBHW031320040426
42443CB00005B/157